Oct 17

WELCOME TO THE FARM

Farm Quad

Samantha Bell

Published in the United States of America
by Cherry Lake Publishing
Ann Arbor, Michigan
www.cherrylakepublishing.com

Content Adviser: Gary Powell, Weed Science Research Technician,
Michigan State University
Reading Adviser: Marla Conn MS, Ed., Literacy specialist, Read-Ability, Inc.
Photo Credits: © mtneer_man/Flickr, cover, 1, 2, 14; © Kzenon/Shutterstock,
4, 20; © Pierdelune/Shutterstock, 6; © ChameleonsEye/Shutterstock, 8;
© logoboom/Shutterstock, 10; © Anne Greenwood/Shutterstock, 12;
© Anna Jurkovska/Shutterstock, 16; © David P. Lewis/Shutterstock, 18

Library of Congress Cataloging-in-Publication Data
Names: Bell, Samantha, author. | Bell, Samantha. Welcome to the farm.
Title: Farm quad / Samantha Bell.
Description: Ann Arbor : Cherry Lake Publishing, [2016] | Series: Welcome
  to the farm | Includes bibliographical references and index.
Identifiers: LCCN 2015047233| ISBN 9781634710404 (hardcover) |
  ISBN 9781634711395 (pdf) | ISBN 9781634712385 (pbk.) |
  ISBN 9781634713375 (ebook)
Subjects: LCSH: Agricultural machinery—Juvenile literature. |
  All terrain vehicles—Juvenile literature.
Classification: LCC S675.25 .B45 2016 | DDC 631.3—dc23
LC record available at http://lccn.loc.gov/2015047233

Cherry Lake Publishing would like to acknowledge the work of the Partnership
for 21st Century Skills. Please visit www.p21.org for more information.

Printed in the United States of America
Corporate Graphics

Table of Contents

3

Going All Over

ATVs are all-**terrain** vehicles. They are also called quads. Many farmers use them.

What season does it look like?

Quads can go all over the farm. They can go across fields. They can go through woods.

Uses for Quads

One or two people can ride a quad. Quads help farmers do their work.

Farmers use quads to get their work done faster, and to travel where they can't drive a truck. They can check on their **crops**.

Why do you think herding cows is important?

They use them to herd **livestock**.

Tools for Quads

Farmers can add tools to quads. This one has a **GPS**. Other quads pull tools to dig through the dirt.

What else do you think
this quad could pull?

Quads can pull wagons. Farmers can move heavy things.

Quads are not only used on farms. Police officers and other people can ride them too.

The Fun Part

The work is finished.
Time to ride for fun!

Find Out More

Anderson, Jenna, and Bob and Diane Wolfe. *How It Happens at the ATV Plant*. Minneapolis: Oliver Press, 2004.

4-H ATV Safety
www.atv-youth.org/
Learn about ATVs and ATV safety.

Glossary

crops (KRAHPS) plants grown as food
GPS (GEE PEE ESS) a digital map system
livestock (LIVE-stahk) farm animals
terrain (tuh-RAYN) the surface of an area of land

Home and School Connection

Use this list of words from the book to help your child become a better reader. Word games and writing activities can help beginning readers reinforce literacy skills.

a	do	heavy	other	time
across	does	help	over	to
add	done	herd	part	too
all	drive	herding	people	tools
all-terrain	else	important	police	travel
also	farm	is	pull	truck
and	farmers	it	quad	two
are	farms	like	quads	use
ATVs	faster	livestock	ride	used
called	fields	look	season	vehicles
can	finished	many	the	wagons
can't	for	move	their	what
check	fun	not	them	where
could	get	officers	they	woods
cows	go	on	things	work
crops	going	one	think	you
dig	GPS	only	this	
dirt	has	or	through	

Index

About the Author

Samantha Bell is a children's book writer, illustrator, teacher, and mom of four busy kids. Her articles, short stories, and poems have been published online and in print.